EVIDENCE–BASED PSYCHOTHERAPY TREATMENT PLANNING

DVD COMPANION WORKBOOK

ARTHUR E. JONGSMA, JR.

AND

TIMOTHY J. BRUCE

WILEY

John Wiley & Sons, Inc.

Table of Contents

Introduction

This *Workbook* is a supplement to the *Evidence-Based Treatment Planning* DVD, which is focused on informing mental health clinicians and addiction counselors about evidence-based psychological treatment.

Organization

In this *Workbook* you will find in each chapter:

➤ Summary highlights of content shown in the DVD
➤ Chapter review questions
➤ Chapter review test questions
➤ Chapter references
➤ Key points

In Appendix A, the correct and incorrect answers to all chapter review test questions are explained.

Chapter Points

This video is electronically marked with chapter points that delineate the beginning of discussion sections throughout the program. You may skip to any one of these chapter points in the video by clicking on the forward arrow. The chapter points for this program are as follows:

➤ History of the Empirically Supported Treatment (EST) Movement
➤ EST and Evidence-Based Practice (EBP)
➤ Advantages of Using ESTs
➤ Limitations of ESTs
➤ Essential Elements of Treatment Planning
➤ Empirically Informed Treatment Planning

Series Rationale

Evidence-based practice (EBP) is steadily becoming the standard of care in mental healthcare, as it has in medical healthcare. Borrowing from the Institute of Medicine's definition (Institute of Medicine, 2001), the American Psychological Association (APA) has defined EBP as "the integration of the best available research with clinical expertise in the context of patient characteristics, culture, and preferences" (American Psychological Association Presidential Task Force on Evidence-Based Practice [APA], 2006).

Professional organizations such as the American Psychological Association, the National Association of Social Workers, and the American Psychiatric Association, as well as consumer organizations such as the National Alliance for the Mentally Ill (NAMI), are endorsing EBP. At the federal level, a major joint initiative of the National Institute of Mental Health and Department of Health and Human Services' Substance Abuse and Mental Health Services Administration (SAMHSA) focuses on promoting, implementing, and evaluating evidence-based mental health programs and practices within state mental health systems (APA, 2006). In some practice settings, EBP is becoming mandated. It is clear that the call for evidence and accountability is being increasingly sounded.

Unfortunately, many mental health care providers cannot or do not stay abreast of results from clinical research and how these results can inform their practices. Although it has rightfully been argued that the relevance of some research to the clinician's needs is weak, there are products of clinical research whose efficacy has been well established and whose effectiveness in the community setting has received support. Clinicians and clinicians-in-training who are interested in empirically informing their treatments could benefit from educational programs that make this goal more easily attainable.

This series of DVDs and companion workbooks is designed to introduce clinicians and students to the process of empirically informing their psychotherapy treatment plans. The series begins with an introduction to the efforts to identify research-supported treatments and to ways that the products of these efforts can be used to inform treatment planning. The other programs in the series focus on empirically informed treatment planning for each of several commonly seen clinical problems. In each problem - focused DVD, issues involved in defining or diagnosing the presenting problem are reviewed. Research-supported treatments for the problem are described, as well as the process used to identify them. Viewers are then systematically guided through the process of creating a treatment plan, and shown how the plan can be informed by goals, objectives, and interventions consistent with those of the identified research-supported treatments. Example vignettes of selected interventions are also provided. This series is intended to be educational and informative in nature and not meant to be a substitute for clinical training in the specific interventions discussed and demonstrated. References to empirical support of the treatments described, clinical resource material, and training opportunities are provided.

Presenters

Exhibit I.1 Dr. Tim Bruce and Dr. Art Jongsma

Dr. Art Jongsma is the Series Editor and coauthor of the Practice*Planners*® series[1] published by John Wiley & Sons. He has authored or coauthored more than 40 books in this series. Among the books included in this series are the highly regarded *The Complete Adult Psychotherapy Treatment Planner, The Adolescent and The Child Psychotherapy Treatment Planners, and The Addiction Treatment Planner*. All of these books, along with *The Severe and Persistent Mental Illness Treatment Planner, The Family Therapy Treatment Planner, The Veterans and Active Duty Military Psychotherapy Treatment Planner, The Couples Psychotherapy Treatment Planner, and The Older Adult Psychotherapy Treatment Planner,* are informed with objectives and interventions that are supported by research evidence.

Dr. Jongsma also created the clinical record management software tool, Thera*Scribe*®, which uses point-and-click technology to easily develop, store, and print treatment plans, progress notes, and homework assignments. He has conducted treatment planning and software training workshops for mental health professionals around the world.

Dr. Jongsma's clinical career began as a psychologist in a large private psychiatric hospital. He worked in the hospital for about 10 years and then transitioned to outpatient work in his own private practice clinic, Psychological Consultants, in Grand Rapids, Michigan for 25 years. He has been writing best-selling books and software for mental health professionals since 1995.

Dr. Timothy Bruce is a Professor and Associate Chair of the Department of Psychiatry and Behavioral Medicine at the University of Illinois, College of Medicine in Peoria, Illinois, where he also directs medical student education. He is a licensed clinical psychologist who completed his graduate training at SUNY–Albany under

---

[1]These books are updated frequently, check with the publisher for the latest editions.

the mentorship of Dr. David Barlow and his residency training at Wilford Hall Medical Center under the direction of Dr. Robert Klepac. In addition to maintaining an active clinical practice at the university, Dr. Bruce has authored numerous publications including books, professional journal articles, book chapters, and professional educational materials, many on the topic of evidence-based practice. Most recently, he has served as the contributing editor empirically informing Dr. Jongsma's best-selling Practice*Planners*® Series.

Dr. Bruce is also Executive Director of the Center for the Dissemination of Evidence-based Mental Health Practices, a state- and federally funded initiative to disseminate evidence-based psychological and pharmacological practices across Illinois. Highly recognized as an educator, Dr. Bruce has received nearly two dozen awards for his teaching of students and professionals during his career.

References

American Psychological Association Presidential Task Force on Evidence-Based Practice. (2006). Evidence-based practice in psychology. *American Psychologist, 61*(4), 271–285.

Berghuis, D., Jongsma, A., & Bruce, T. (2006). *The severe and persistent mental illness treatment planner* (2nd ed.). Hoboken, NJ: John Wiley & Sons.

Dattilio, F., Jongsma, A., & Davis, S. (2009). *The family therapy treatment planner* (2nd ed.). Hoboken, NJ: John Wiley & Sons.

Institute of Medicine. (2001). *Crossing the quality chasm: A new health system for the 21st century.* Washington, DC: National Academy Press

Jongsma, A., Peterson, M., & Bruce, T. (2006). *The complete adult psychotherapy treatment planner* (4th ed.). Hoboken, NJ: John Wiley & Sons.

Jongsma, A., Peterson, M., McInnis, W., & Bruce, T. (2006a). *The adolescent psychotherapy treatment planner* (4th ed.). Hoboken, NJ: John Wiley & Sons.

Jongsma, A., Peterson, M., McInnis, W., & Bruce, T. (2006b). *The child psychotherapy treatment planner* (4th ed.). Hoboken, NJ: John Wiley & Sons.

Moore, B., & Jongsma, A. (2009). *The veterans and active duty military psychotherapy treatment planner.* Hoboken, NJ: John Wiley & Sons.

Perkinson, R., Jongsma, A., & Bruce, T. (2009). *The addiction treatment planner* (4th ed.). Hoboken, NJ: John Wiley & Sons.

CHAPTER 1

What is the Brief History of the Empirically Supported Treatments Movement?

In the United States, the effort to identify empirically supported treatments (EST) began with an initiative of the American Psychological Association's Division 12— The Society of Clinical Psychology.

In 1993, APA's Division 12 President, David Barlow, initiated a task group, chaired by Diane Chambless, whose charge was to review the psychotherapy outcome literature to identify psychological treatments whose efficacy had been demonstrated through clinical research.

This group was originally called the Task Force on the Promotion and Dissemination of Psychological Procedures. The subsequent iteration of it was renamed the Task Force on Psychological Interventions. Note: On the DVD, our reference to the Task Force on Psychological Interventions refers to the work of both task groups.

Process Used to Identify ESTs

In evaluating the psychotherapy outcome literature, these reviewers first established two primary sets of criteria for judging the evidence base supporting any particular therapy. One was termed *well-established*, the other *probably efficacious*. Figure 1.1 illustrates the criteria for both well-established, and probably efficacious treatments.

Products of EST Reviews

The products of these reviews can be found in the Division 12 groups' final two reports.

- ➤ In the first, 47 ESTs are identified (Chambless et al., 1996).
- ➤ In the final, the list had grown to 71 ESTs (Chambless et al., 1998).

─────── **Figure 1.1** ───────

Specific Criteria for Well-Established and Probably Efficacious Treatments

Criteria for Well-Established Treatments

For a psychological treatment to be considered *well-established*, the evidence base supporting it had to be characterized by the following:

I. At least two good between group design experiments demonstrating efficacy in one or more of the following ways:

   A. Superior (statistically significantly so) to pill or psychological placebo or to another treatment
   B. Equivalent to an already established treatment in experiments with adequate sample sizes

OR

II. A large series of single case design experiments (n > 9) demonstrating efficacy. These experiments must have:

   A. Used good experimental designs
   B. Compared the intervention to another treatment as in IA

Further Criteria for Both I and II

III. Experiments must be conducted with treatment manuals.

IV. Characteristics of the client samples must be clearly specified.

V. Effects must have been demonstrated by at least two different investigators or investigating teams.

Criteria for Probably Efficacious Treatments

For a psychological treatment to be considered *probably efficacious*, the evidence base supporting it had to meet the following criteria:

I. Two experiments showing the treatment is superior (statistically significantly so) to a waiting-list control group.

OR

II. One or more experiments meeting the well-established treatment criteria IA or IB, III, and IV, but not V.

OR

III. A small series of single case design experiments (n > 3) otherwise meeting well-established treatment criteria.

Adapted from: Chambless, D. L., Baker, M. J., Baucom, D. H., Beutler, L. E., Calhoun, K. S., Crits-Christoph, P., Daiuto, A., DeRubeis, R., Detweiler, J., Haaga, D. A. F., Bennett Johnson, S., McCurry, S., Mueser, K. T., Pope, K. S., Sanderson, W. C., Shoham, V., Stickle, T., Williams, D. A., & Woody, S. R. (1998). Update on empirically validated therapies, II. *The Clinical Psychologist, 51*, 3–16.

➤ In 1999, The Society of Clinical Psychology, Division 12, took full ownership of maintaining the growing list. The current list and information center can be found on its Web site, at www.psychologicaltreatments.org.

Around this same time, other groups emerged, using the same or similar criteria, to review literatures related to other populations, problems, and interventions. Examples include the following:

➤ Children (Lonigan & Elbert, 1998)
➤ Pediatric Psychology (Spirito, 1999)
➤ Older Adults (Gatz et al., 1998)
➤ Adult, Child, Marital, Family Therapy (Kendall & Chambless, 1998).
➤ Psychopharmacology and Psychological Treatments (Nathan & Gorman, 1998; 2002; 2007)
➤ For those interested in comparing and contrasting the criteria used by various review groups, see Chambless and Ollendick (2001).

Other Organizational Reviewers of Evidence-Based Psychological Treatments

➤ Great Britain was at the forefront of the effort to identify evidence-based treatments and develop guidelines for practice. The latest products of their work can be found at the Web site for the National Institute for Health and Clinical Excellence (NICE): www.nice.org.uk.
➤ The Substance Abuse and Mental Health Service Administration (SAMHSA) has also begun an initiative to evaluate, identify, and provide information on various mental health practices. Their work, entitled "The National Registry of Evidence-based Programs and Practices," can also be found online at www.nrepp.samhsa.gov.

Key Point

The Web site www.therapyadvisor.com provides descriptions, references to empirical support, clinical training materials, and training opportunities for many of the empirically supported treatments identified by the original Division 12 review groups.

Chapter Review

1. How did Division 12 of the APA identify empirically supported treatments?
2. What are the primary differences between well-established and probably efficacious criteria used to identify ESTs?
3. Where can information about ESTs and evidence-based practices be found?

Chapter Review Test Questions

1. Which statement best describes the process used to identify ESTs?

    A. Consumers of mental health services nominated therapies.
    B. Experts came to a consensus based on their experiences with the treatments.
    C. Researchers submitted their works.
    D. Task groups reviewed the literature using clearly defined selection criteria for ESTs.

2. Based on the differences in their criteria, in which of the following ways are *well-established* treatments different from those classified as *probably efficacious*?

    A. Only probably efficacious treatments allowed the use of a single case design experiments.
    B. Only well-established treatments allowed studies comparing the treatment to a psychological placebo.
    C. Only well-established treatments required demonstration by at least two different, independent investigators or investigating teams.
    D. Only well-established treatments allowed studies comparing the treatment to a pill placebo.

Chapter References

Chambless, D. L., & Ollendick, T. H. (2001). Empirically supported psychological interventions: Controversies and evidence. *Annual Review of Psychology, 52,* 685–716.

Chambless, D. L., Sanderson, W. C., Shoham, V., Bennett Johnson, S., Pope, K. S., Crits-Christoph, P., Baker, M., Johnson, B., Woody, S. R., Sue, S., Beutler, L., Williams, D. A., & McCurry, S. (1996). An update on empirically validated therapies. *The Clinical Psychologist, 49,* 5–18.

Chambless, D. L., Baker, M. J., Baucom, D. H., Beutler, L. E., Calhoun, K. S., Crits-Christoph, P., Daiuto, A., DeRubeis, R., Detweiler, J., Haaga, D. A. F., Bennett Johnson, S., McCurry, S., Mueser, K. T., Pope, K. S., Sanderson, W. C., Shoham, V., Stickle, T., Williams, D. A., & Woody, S. R. (1998). Update on empirically validated therapies, II. *The Clinical Psychologist, 51(1),* 3–16.

Gatz, M., Fiske, A., Fox, L. S., Kaskie, B., Kasl-Godley, J. E., et al. (1998). Empirically validated psychological treatments for older adults. *Journal of Mental Health and Aging, 41,* 9–46.

Kendall, P. C., & Chambless, D. L. (Eds.). (1998). Empirically supported psychological therapies [Special issue]. *Journal of Consulting and Clinical Psychology, 66(3),* 151–167.

Lonigan, C. J., & Elbert, J. C. (Eds.). (1998). Special issue on empirically supported psychosocial interventions for children. *Journal of Clinical Child Psychology, 27,* 138–226.

Nathan, P. E., & Gorman, J. M. (Eds.). (1998). *A guide to treatments that work.* New York: Oxford University Press.

Nathan, P. E., & Gorman, J. M. (Eds.). (2002*). A guide to treatments that work* (2nd ed.). New York: Oxford University Press.

Nathan, P. E., & Gorman, J. M. (Eds.). (2007). *A guide to treatments that work* (3rd ed.). New York: Oxford University Press.

Spirito, A. (Ed.). (1999). Empirically supported treatments in pediatric psychology [Special issue]. *Journal of Pediatric Psychology, 24,* 87–174.

2

How Are Empirically Supported Treatments Related to Evidence-Based Practice?

Empirically supported treatments (ESTs) are treatments whose efficacy has been demonstrated through clinical research.

Evidence-based practice (EBP) is broader in concept than EST in that it includes consideration of factors such as assessment, case formulation, client and therapist characteristics, and the therapeutic relationship, in addition to the specific EST used.

The APA's definition of EBP reflects the broader scope of EBP: "Integration of the best available research with clinical expertise, in the context of patient characteristics, culture, and preferences" (American Psychological Association Presidential Task Force on Evidence-Based Practice [APA], 2006, p. 273).

> Research has shown that the treatment method (Nathan & Gorman, 2002), the individual psychologist (Wampold, 2001), the treatment relationship (Norcross, 2002), and the patient (Bohart & Tallman, 1999) are all vital contributors to the success of psychological practice. Comprehensive evidence-based practice will consider all of these determinants and their optimal combinations. (APA, 2006, p. 275)

Clients' characteristics, such as functional status, readiness to change, and level of social support (Norcross, 2002), influence treatment outcome. Other patient variables are important to treatment outcome:

> ➤ "Variations in presenting problems or disorders, etiology, concurrent symptoms or syndromes, and behavior;
> ➤ Chronological age, developmental status, developmental history, and life stage;
> ➤ Sociocultural and familial factors (e.g., gender, gender identity, ethnicity, race, social class, religion, disability status, family structure, and sexual orientation);

➢ Current environmental context, stressors (e.g., unemployment or recent life event), and social factors (e.g., institutional racism and healthcare disparities);

➢ Personal preferences, values, and preferences related to treatment (e.g., goals, beliefs, worldviews, and treatment expectations)." (APA, 2006, p. 279)

Key Point

It is important to recognize that although this treatment planning series, by its nature, places emphasis on the content of therapy, such as its objectives and treatment interventions, other factors, such as those of the client, the therapist, and the therapeutic relationship, have been shown to contribute to therapeutic outcome as well and should obviously be considered in the delivery of any psychotherapy treatment plan.

Chapter Review

1. What is an empirically supported treatment (EST)?
2. To what does the term evidence-based practice (EBP) refer?
3. How are ESTs and EBP related?

Chapter Review Test Questions

1. Which statement best summarizes the difference between empirically supported treatments (ESTs) and evidence-based practice (EBP).

   A. EBP and ESTs are two labels describing the same thing.
   B. EBP focuses on therapeutic relationship factors, ESTs focus on the content of therapy.
   C. EBP does not integrate research results, ESTs do.
   D. EBP is broader in scope than ESTs.

2. Although the effective delivery of an empirically informed psychological treatment plan involves consideration of several factors, including those related to the client, the therapist, their relationship, and the interventions used, the written treatment plan, by its nature, places emphasis on describing which of the following:

   A. The client factors
   B. The relationship factors
   C. The therapist factors
   D. The treatment interventions

Chapter References

American Psychological Association Presidential Task Force on Evidence-Based Practice. (2006). Evidence-based practice in psychology. *American Psychologist, 61*(4), 271–285.

Bohart, A., & Tallman, K. (1999). *How clients make therapy work: The process of active self-healing.* Washington, DC: American Psychological Association.

Nathan, P. E., & Gorman, J. M. (2002). *A guide to treatments that work.* London: Oxford University Press.

Norcross, J. C. (Ed.). (2002). *Psychotherapy relationships that work: Therapist contributions and responsiveness to patient needs.* New York: Oxford University Press.

Wampold, B. E. (2001). *The great psychotherapy debate: Models, methods, and findings.* Mahwah, NJ: Lawrence Erlbaum.

CHAPTER **3**

What Are the Advantages of Using Empirically Supported Treatments?

Advantages of using empirically informed treatments (ESTs) have been identified at different levels of the psychotherapy service delivery system.

To the Client

➢ Participation in an empirically informed therapy increases confidence that there will be a clinical benefit.
➢ Facilitates a positive expectation of successful treatment because the interventions planned have shown efficacy.

To the Clinician

➢ Promotes accountability in that the clinician is using interventions that are selected based on research evidence.
➢ Ensures ethical treatment, as the clinician has a solid basis for the treatment rationale.
➢ Is practical, as it keeps treatment focused and structured based on manuals or specific intervention guidelines for implementation.
➢ May provide some protection from malpractice claims, as the treatment plan is scientifically based.

To the Agency

➢ Use of empirically informed treatment supports most agencies' goal of delivering quality care.
➢ It satisfies quality assurance standards.
➢ It makes the agency more competitive in the marketplace.
➢ Reimbursement rates increase as demands of payors for use of evidence-based practice are met.

To the Profession

➢ Bring potentially effective treatments to practitioners in the community setting; help to close the "scientist-practitioner gap."

➣ Improves the reputation of "therapy" in the healthcare field, as efficacy has been studied scientifically and supported.

➣ Justifies future funding of clinical research as the results are brought to practical usefulness and human benefit.

To National Policy

➣ Advances the mental health agenda for improved client care.

➣ Increases societal respect for the profession, which increases the profession's ability to influence policy.

Chapter Review

1. How can the use of empirically informed treatment benefit clients, clinicians, agencies, the profession, and national policy?

Chapter Review Test Questions

1. The potential advantages of using ESTs are:

   A. Found across several levels of the psychotherapy service delivery system
   B. Primarily for clinicians, through malpractice protection
   C. Primarily for agencies, through improved business competitiveness
   D. Primarily for clients, through the previous demonstration of efficacy

2. One of the advantages of using ESTs is that it may help close the *scientist-practitioner gap*. The gap in this sense refers to what?

   A. The dissemination of clinical research findings to community treatment settings
   B. The theoretical orientations of researchers and practitioners
   C. The training backgrounds of researchers and practitioners
   D. The types of clinical problems seen in both settings

Chapter References

American Psychological Association Presidential Task Force on Evidence-Based Practice. (2006). Evidence-based practice in psychology. *American Psychologist*, 61(4), 271–285.

4

What Are the Limitations of Identified Empirically Supported Treatments?

The movement to identify empirically supported treatments (ESTs) has been met with some criticism. In this chapter, we highlight a few primary concerns with the effort to identify ESTs.

Levels of Evidence

The levels of evidence supporting ESTs are not equally advanced.

Key Point

To understand the implications of this point, it is helpful to understand the difference between studies evaluating *efficacy*, *effectiveness*, and *utility* (see APA, 2006; Hoagwood, Hibbs, Brent, & Jensen, 1995).

Efficacy

Efficacy refers to the systematic and scientific evaluation of whether a treatment works. Efficacy studies aim to control for alternative explanations of a therapeutic outcome. A randomized, placebo-controlled trial is an example of an efficacy study. These studies are designed to identify whether a positive outcome is achieved and, ideally, whether it is due to the unique features of the therapy under investigation.

Literatures supporting ESTs that contain a number of high-quality efficacy studies are in a better position to conclude that the treatment is actually efficacious and that this efficacy is due specifically to the treatment intervention under study.

Effectiveness

While efficacy studies strive to test whether and why a treatment works, effectiveness studies test whether a treatment's efficacy extends to the clinic settings with natural client populations. That is, they evaluate the therapy's effectiveness in real-world application, including client satisfaction with the therapy.

A treatment showing efficacy for a particular problem with a particular sample of clients in a research study may or may not show similar efficacy when delivered to clients in the natural setting with all of its complexities.

Effectiveness studies test whether treatment effects *generalize*, or are *transportable*, to the natural community setting in which most are delivered.

Utility

Utility, or clinical utility, is an extension of effectiveness.

It refers to the applicability, feasibility, and practical usefulness of an intervention in the local or specific setting where it is offered.

Examples of utility considerations might include the evaluation of costs to implement the treatment, training requirements for staff, and ease of documentation.

Key Points

- The criteria used to identify ESTs have focused on demonstrations of their efficacy, not necessarily their effectiveness or utility.
- While literatures supporting some ESTs have advanced to where effectiveness demonstrations are evident, others have not. That is, the effectiveness and utility of some ESTs have not been demonstrated.

It is important to note that this state of affairs is not an unplanned outcome of the EST movement, but rather a demonstration that it is a work in progress. The following quote from the original Division 12 group captures this point:

> The content of this list [of ESTs] is restricted in at least two notable ways: First, our focus is on what is often termed *efficacy* rather than *effectiveness*. That is, we concentrate here on demonstrations that a treatment is beneficial for patients or clients in well-controlled treatment studies. Effectiveness studies are of importance as well; these include studies of how well an efficacious treatment can be transported from the research clinic to community and private practice settings. Once the task force has more comprehensively covered the efficacy literature, we expect to broach the subject of effectiveness. (Chambless et al., 1998, p. 3)

Today, most major federally funded studies of psychotherapies attend to effectiveness considerations in their designs.

It is notable that studies attending to effectiveness concerns are becoming more prevalent in the literature and that many are supportive of the generalizability of ESTs (e.g., Chambless & Ollendick, 2001; Stewart & Chambless, in press).

That support must also be qualified, as some effectiveness studies have shown positive outcome, but not without some differences from the outcome of original efficacy studies. Examples include higher dropout rates in community studies compared to the efficacy studies (e.g., Wade et al. 1998), or longer treatment (e.g., Persons, 1998a). Some studies report improvement in clients, but not at the level or overall quality of response seen in efficacy studies (e.g., Organista et al., 1994; Sanderson et al., 1998).

Downplaying Other Factors

The effort to identify ESTs downplays the importance of other factors involved in the delivery of psychotherapy, some of which have been shown to contribute to therapeutic outcome. Examples include factors related to the client, the therapist, and their relationship.

As noted in Chapter 2 of this workbook (see p. 6), research has shown that the treatment method, the individual psychologist, the treatment relationship, and the client are all vital contributors to the success of psychological practice (see APA, 2006).

The EST review groups acknowledge that their efforts are only part of the equation in determining therapeutic outcome. That is directly reflected in this statement by Division 12 on its Web site disseminating information of research supported treatments. It states that,

> The client, the therapist, and the therapeutic relationship are among factors that also contribute to effective treatment. In providing information on research-supported psychological treatments we do not intend to devalue the importance of these other factors. (www.psychologicaltreatments.org)

In response to this limitation on identifying ESTs, an effort was undertaken by the Psychotherapy Division of the APA (Division 29) to identify empirically supported relationship variables (ESRs). For more on this work, see these works of John Norcross (2001, 2002).

Integrating ESTs and ESRs

> I think it's fair to say that although early discussions of these issues were the topic of sometimes polarizing debate, recent attempts have been made to look at how content, process, and other factors can be brought into an evidence-based practice that reflects their contributions. (Dr. Art Jongsma, in this DVD)

Key Point

Recent attempts to integrate the various factors that influence the outcome of psychotherapy are reflected in the movement to identify *principles* of therapeutic change that reflect contributions from the EST and ESR movements. Several authors have written about this. A good starting place is the work of Castonguay and Beutler (2006).

This type of integration is what is reflected in APA's definition of the evidence-based practice of psychology, which states:

> . . . The integration of the best available research with clinical expertise in the context of patient characteristics, culture, and preferences . . . (APA, 2006, p. 273)

What Can the Clinician Do Toward the Goal of Having an EBP?

Key Points

RECOMMENDATIONS FOR ADVANCING AN EVIDENCE-BASED PRACTICE
- Conduct a thorough assessment/diagnostics/case formulation.
- Stay up on the EST and ESR literature and its potential application to your clients.
- Empirically inform your treatment with applicable ESTs.
- Select and deliver treatment with sensitivity toward ESR considerations.
- Continuously monitor outcomes.
- Use a scientist-practitioner, hypothesis-testing approach to maximize outcome.

For more thorough discussion of this topic, see APA (2006).

Chapter Review

1. What is the limitation of ESTs related to levels of evidence?
2. How do efficacy and effectiveness differ?
3. The effort to identify ESTs has been criticized on the basis that it excludes what type of other considerations related to therapeutic outcome?
4. What can clinicians do to foster an evidence-based practice?

Chapter Review Test Questions

1. An investigator is developing a new psychotherapy and wants to see if it performs better than a wait-list control condition. This type of study is typically used in the process of establishing the therapy's . . .

   A. Effectiveness
   B. Efficacy
   C. Transportability
   D. Utility

2. Which of the following best characterizes one of the criticisms of the evidence base supporting most ESTs?

   A. Effectiveness studies are overrepresented.
   B. Effectiveness studies are underrepresented.
   C. Efficacy studies are overrepresented.
   D. Efficacy studies are underrepresented.

Chapter References

American Psychological Association Presidential Task Force on Evidence-Based Practice. (2006). Evidence-based practice in psychology. *American Psychologist, 61*(4), 271–285.

Castonguay, L. G., & Beutler, L. E. (Eds.) (2006). *Empirically supported principles of therapy change.* New York: Oxford University Press.

Chambless, D. L., Baker, M. J., Baucom, D. H., Beutler, L. E., Calhoun, K. S., Crits-Christoph, P., et al. (1998). Update on empirically validated therapies, II. *The Clinical Psychologist, 51*(1), 3–16.

Chambless, D. L., & Ollendick, T. H. (2001). Empirically supported psychological interventions: Controversies and evidence. *Annual Review of Psychology, 52,* 685–716.

Hoagwood, K., Hibbs, E., Brent, D., & Jensen, P. (1995). Introduction to the special section: Efficacy and effectiveness in studies of child and adolescent psychotherapy. *Journal of Consulting and Clinical Psychology, 63,* 683–687.

Norcross, J. C. (2001). Purposes, processes, and products of the task force on empirically supported therapy relationships. *Journal of the Division of Psychotherapy, American Psychological Association, 38,* 345–356.

Norcross, J. C. (Ed.). (2002). *Psychotherapy relationships that work: therapist contributions and responsiveness to patient needs.* New York: Oxford University Press.

Organista, K. C., Munoz, R. F., & Gonzalez, G. (1994). Cognitive-behavioral therapy for depression in low-income and minority medial outpatients: Description of a program and exploratory analyses. *Cognitive Therapy and Research, 18,* 241–259.

Persons, J. B., Bostrom, A., & Bertagnolli, A. (1999). Results of randomized controlled trials of cognitive therapy for depression generalize to private practice. *Cognitive Therapy and Research, 23*, 535–548.

Sanderson, W. C., Raue, P. J., & Wetzler, S. (1998). The generalizability of cognitive behavior therapy for panic disorder. *Journal of Cognitive Psychotherapy, 12*, 323–330.

Stewart, R. E., & Chambless, D. L. (2009). Cognitive-behavioral therapy for adult anxiety disorders in clinical practice: A meta-analysis of effectiveness studies. *Journal of Consulting and Clinical Psychology, 77*, 595–606.

For More on These Topics

APA Task Force on Evidence-Based Practice for Children and Adolescents. (2008). *Disseminating evidence-based practice for children and adolescents: A systems approach to enhancing care.* Washington, DC: American Psychological Association.

Bruce, T. J., & Sanderson, W. C. (2005). Evidence-based psychosocial practices: Past, present, and future. In C. Stout & R. Hayes (Eds.), *The evidence-based practice: Methods, models, and tools for mental health professionals* (pp. 220–243). Hoboken, NJ: John Wiley & Sons.

Chorpita, B. F. (2003). The frontier of evidence-based practice. In A. E. Kazdin & J. R. Weisz (Eds.), *Evidence-based psychotherapies for children and adolescents* (pp. 42–59). NY: Guilford.

Chu, B. C. Comparing empirically supported treatments and evidence-based practice. A public domain, PowerPoint presentation by Brian C. Chu, Ph.D., available online at: www.abct.org/docs/dMental/Slides/ComparingESTsEBPChuRutgers.ppt

Sanderson, W. C. (2003). Why empirically supported psychological treatments are important. *Behavior Modification, 27*, 290–299.

Wampold, B. E. (2001). *The great psychotherapy debate: Models, methods, and findings.* Mahwah, NJ: Lawrence Erlbaum.

Wampold, B. E., Lichtengberg, J. W., & Waehler, C. A. (2002). Principles of empirically supported interventions in counseling psychology. *The Counseling Psychologist, 30*, 197–217.

5

What Are the Six Steps in Building a Treatment Plan?

Step 1: Identify primary and secondary problems
➤ Use evidence-based psychosocial assessment procedures to determine the most significant problem, making sure to include client input as to pain and disruption in functioning.

Step 2: Describe the problem's behavioral manifestations (symptom pattern)
➤ Note how the problem symptoms reveal themselves in your unique client.

Step 3: Make a diagnosis based on DSM/ICD criteria
➤ Determine the appropriate diagnosis using the process and criteria from the DSM or ICD.

Step 4: Specify long-term goals
➤ These are broad statements describing the anticipated end result of treatment.

Step 5: Create short-term objectives
➤ Objectives for the client to achieve should be stated in measurable or observable terms so accountability is enhanced.

Step 6: Select therapeutic interventions
➤ At least one interventional action to be implemented by the therapist should be paired with each client objective to assist the client in reaching that specific objective.

Sample Treatment Plan

Primary Problem: Depression

BEHAVIORAL DEFINITIONS (SYMPTOMS/MANIFESTATIONS)

1. Sad thoughts and affect

(continues)

2. Decreased interest

3. Lack of energy

4. Difficulty concentrating or decision making

5. Decreased appetite

6. Sleep disturbance

LONG-TERM GOAL

1. Alleviate depressive symptoms and return to previous level of effective functioning.

Short-Term Objectives	Therapeutic Interventions
1. Identify and replace cognitive self-talk that is engaged in to support depression.	1. Assign the client to keep a daily journal of automatic thoughts associated with depressive feelings; process the journal material to challenge depressive thinking patterns and replace them with reality-based thoughts.
2. Utilize behavioral strategies to overcome depression.	1. Engage the client in *behavioral activation* by scheduling activities that have a high likelihood for pleasure and mastery; use rehearsal, role-playing, role-reversal, as needed, to assist adoption in the client's daily life, reinforcing success.
3. Increase assertive communication.	2. Use modeling and/or role-playing to train the client in assertiveness; if indicated, refer him/her to an assertiveness training class for further instruction.

DIAGNOSIS

(296.22) Major Depressive Disorder, Single Episode, Moderate

Key Point

Effective treatment planning requires that each plan is tailored to the individual client's unique problems and needs. Treatment plans should not be boilerplate, even if clients have similar problems. Consistent with the definition of an evidence-based practice in psychology advanced by the American Psychological Association Presidential Task Force on Evidence-Based Practice (APA, 2006), the individual's strengths and weaknesses, unique stressors, cultural and social network family circumstances, and symptom patterns must be considered in developing a treatment strategy. Clinicians should rely on their own good clinical judgment and select interventions that are appropriate for the distinctive individual with whom they are working.

Chapter Review

1. What are the six steps involved in developing a psychotherapy treatment plan.

Chapter Review Test Questions

1. A psychotherapy treatment plan can be drawn up without a diagnosis. For example, a good case formulation can be the basis of therapy. Why is it important to consider the diagnosis when developing a plan that could be informed by ESTs?

   A. A diagnosis is necessary to judge response to the EST.
   B. It is not necessary to consider diagnosis in empirically informed treatment planning.
   C. Some ESTs were developed and studied using diagnosis as inclusion criteria.
   D. Treatment may require medication, which typically requires diagnosis to be specified.

2. The statement, "Identify, challenge, and change biased self-talk supportive of depression" is an example of which of the following steps in a treatment plan?

   A. A primary problem
   B. A short-term objective
   C. A symptom manifestation
   D. A treatment intervention

Chapter References

American Psychological Association Presidential Task Force on Evidence-Based Practice. (2006). Evidence-based practice in psychology. *American Psychologist*, *61(4)*, 271–185.

Jongsma, A. (2005). Psychotherapy treatment plan writing. In G. P. Koocher, J. C. Norcross, & S. S. Hill (Eds.), *Psychologists' desk reference* (2nd ed., pp. 232–236). New York: Oxford University Press.

Jongsma, A., Peterson, M., & Bruce, T. (2006). *The complete adult psychotherapy treatment planner* (4th ed.). Hoboken, NJ: Wiley.

6

How Do You Integrate Empirically Supported Treatments into Treatment Planning?

Empirically informing a treatment plan involves integrating those aspects of identified empirically supported treatments (ESTs) for the problem into each step of the treatment planning process. It is important to keep in mind the relationship between empirically informed treatment planning and its implementation. Consistent with the concept of EBP, implementing an empirically informed treatment plan must be done within a context considering important client, therapist, and therapeutic relationship factors.

Empirically Informed Treatment Planning Process

1. An empirically informed treatment plan begins like any treatment plan, by first identifying your client's primary problem. In our sample plan, the primary problem was *depression*.
2. Next, you want to specify exactly how the problem is manifested in the client's life—his or her expression of the problem—known as its behavioral definition.

Behavioral Definition

The behavioral definition statements describe *how the problem manifests itself in the client*. The behavioral definition of depression for your client will be unique and specific to your client. Your assessment will need to identify the symptoms of depression that characterize your client's presentation. The behavioral definition statements for depression closely follow those that are provided in the DSM or ICD. Examples of common definition statements for depression are the following:

➤ Persistently depressed or irritable mood
➤ Diminished interest in or enjoyment of activities
➤ Social withdrawal

- Feelings of hopelessness, worthlessness, or inappropriate guilt
- Lack of energy or fatigue
- Poor concentration and indecisiveness
- Loss of appetite and/or weight
- Psychomotor agitation or retardation
- Insomnia or hypersomnia
- Suicidal thoughts and/or gestures
- Low self-esteem
- Unresolved grief issues
- History of depression for which the client has taken antidepressant medication, been hospitalized, had outpatient treatment, or had a course of electroconvulsive therapy
- Others

For our sample plan, the behavioral definitions were:
- Sad thoughts and affect
- Decreased interest
- Lack of energy
- Difficulty concentrating and decision making
- Decreased appetite
- Sleep disturbance.

3. When you have identified the client's problem, you must determine if it has been the subject of an EST study. For our example of depression, we know that cognitive and behavioral therapies are identified ESTs, in addition to others.
   - Matching an EST to a client involves several considerations including the level of evidence, the match between the client and participants in the studies supporting the EST, and the therapist's expertise in the EST.
   - There are various resources clinicians can use to inform these decisions. Some of the more convenient of these for busy clinicians include the following Web sites:
   - The Web site www.therapyadvisor.com provides descriptions, references to empirical support, clinical training materials, and training opportunities for many of the empirically supported treatment identified by the original Division 12 review groups.
   - For the most recent listing of ESTs, including clinical resources, and training opportunities see The Society of Clinical Psychology's Web site on Research-Supported Psychological Treatments at: www.psychologicaltreatments.org.
   - For practice guidelines, review the Web site for the National Institute for Health and Clinical Excellence (NICE): www.nice.org.uk.

✓➤ For more comprehensive information evidence-based programs and practices, including client characteristics and levels of evidence, visit the Web site of the National Registry of Evidence-based Programs and Practices, at: www.nrepp. samhsa.gov.

4. Having identified an empirically supported treatment relevant to your client's primary problem, the next steps involve identifying goals, objectives and therapist interventions that are consistent with those of the identified ESTs.

Goals

Goals are broad statements describing what you and the client would like *the result of therapy* to be. One statement may suffice, but more than one can be used in the treatment plan. Examples of common goal statements for depression are the following:

➤ Alleviate depressive symptoms and return to previous level of effective functioning.
➤ Recognize, accept, and cope with feelings of depression.
➤ Develop healthy and adaptive cognitive patterns and beliefs about self, others, the world, and the future that lead to alleviation and help prevent the relapse of depression.
➤ Develop healthy and adaptive interpersonal relationships that lead to alleviation and help prevent the relapse of depression symptoms.
➤ Appropriately grieve the loss in order to normalize mood and to return to previous adaptive level of functioning.
➤ Others

In our sample, we chose the following long-term goal, which is consistent with the goals and outcomes measured in our EST:

➤ Alleviate depressive symptoms and return to previous level of effective functioning.

Objectives and Interventions

Objectives are statements that describe small observable *steps the client must achieve* toward attaining the goal of successful treatment. Intervention statements describe the *actions taken by the therapist* to assist the client in achieving his/her objectives. Each objective must be paired with at least one intervention.

We then chose short-term objectives and treatment interventions consistent with our EST including the third, optional objective and intervention, which is relevant to our client. They are as follows:

Short-Term Objectives	Therapeutic Interventions
1. Identify and replace cognitive self-talk that is engaged in to support depression.	1. Assign the client to keep a daily journal of automatic thoughts associated with depressive feelings; process the journal material to challenge depressive thinking patterns and replace them with reality-based thoughts.
2. Utilize behavioral strategies to overcome depression.	2. Engage the client in *behavioral activation* by scheduling activities that have a high likelihood for pleasure and mastery; use rehearsal, role-playing, and role reversal, as needed, to assist adoption in the client's daily life, reinforcing success.
3. Increase assertive communication.	3. Use modeling and/or role-playing to train the client in assertiveness; if indicated, refer him/her to an assertiveness training class for further instruction.

As mentioned on the DVD, it's important to be aware that the research support for any particular EST supports the identified treatment as it was delivered in the studies supporting it. The use of only selected objectives or interventions from ESTs may not be empirically supported.

Key Point

If you want to incorporate an EST into your treatment plan, it should reflect the major objectives and interventions of the approach. Note that in addition to their primary objectives and interventions, many ESTs have options within them that may or may not be used depending on the client's need (e.g., skills training). Most treatment manuals, books, and other training programs identify the primary objectives and interventions used in the EST.

Chapter Review

1. What other consideration should the clinician take into account when implementing an empirically informed treatment plan?
2. What is involved in empirically informing a treatment plan with ESTs?
3. What is the problem with picking and choosing only selected aspects of an EST for a treatment plan versus selecting all of its primary objectives and interventions?

Chapter Review Test Questions

1. Which of the following best describes the practice of incorporating only selected objectives and interventions from ESTs in treatment planning?

   A. It is an empirically supported way to tailor the EST to the client.
   B. It is how ESTs should be integrated into a treatment plan.

    C. It is recommended as a useful means to shorting treatment length.

    D. It may not be an empirically supported use of ESTs.

2. The statement, "Engage the client in *behavioral activation* by scheduling activities that have a high likelihood for pleasure and mastery," is an example of which of the following steps in a treatment plan?

    A. A primary problem

    B. A short-term objective

    C. A symptom manifestation

    D. A treatment intervention

Closing Remarks and Resources

As we note on the DVD, it is important to be aware that the research support for any particular empirically supported treatment (EST) supports the identified treatment as it was delivered in the studies supporting it. The use of only selected objectives or interventions from ESTs may not be empirically supported.

If you want to incorporate an EST into your treatment plan, it should reflect the major objectives and interventions of the approach. Note that in addition to their primary objectives and interventions, many ESTs have options within them that may or may not be used depending on the client's need (e.g., skills training).

Most treatment manuals, books, and other training programs identify the primary objectives and interventions used in the EST. Of course, in accordance with ethical guidelines, therapists should have competency in the services they deliver.

An existing resource for integrating research-supported treatments into treatment planning is the Practice*Planner*® series[1] of *Treatment Planners*. The series contains several books that have integrated goals, objectives, and interventions consistent with those of identified ESTs into treatment plans for several applicable problems and disorders:

> ➤ *The Severe and Persistent Mental Illness Treatment Planner* (Berghuis, Jongsma, & Bruce).
> ➤ *The Family Therapy Treatment Planner* (Dattilio, Jongsma, & Davis)
> ➤ *The Complete Adult Psychotherapy Treatment Planner* (Jongsma, Peterson, & Bruce)
> ➤ *The Adolescent Psychotherapy Treatment Planner* (Jongsma, Peterson, McInnis, & Bruce).

---

[1]These books are updated frequently, check with the publisher for the latest editions, and information about the Practice*Planner*® series.

➤ *The Child Psychotherapy Treatment Planner* (Jongsma, Peterson, McInnis & Bruce).

➤ *The Veterans and Active Duty Military Psychotherapy Treatment Planner* (Moore & Jongsma)

➤ *The Addiction Treatment Planner* (Perkinson, Jongsma, & Bruce)

➤ *The Couples Psychotherapy Treatment Planner* (O'Leary, Heyman, & Jongsma)

Finally, it is important to remember that the purpose of this series is to demonstrate the process of empirically informed psychotherapy treatment planning for common mental health problems. It is designed to be informational in nature and does not intend to be a substitute for clinical training in the interventions discussed and demonstrated. Of course, in accordance with ethical guidelines, therapists should have competency in the services they deliver.

A

Chapter Review Test Question Answers Explained

Chapter 1: What Is the Brief History of the Empirically Supported Treatments Movement?

1. Which statement best describes the process used to identify ESTs?

   A. Consumers of mental health services nominated therapies.
   B. Experts came to a consensus based on their experiences with the treatments.
   C. Researchers submitted their works.
   D. Task groups reviewed the literature using clearly defined selection criteria for ESTs.

   A. *Incorrect*: Mental health professionals selected ESTs.
   B. *Incorrect*: Expert consensus was not the method used to identify ESTs.
   C. *Incorrect*: Empirical works in the existing literature were reviewed to identify ESTs.
   D. *Correct*: Review groups consisting of mental health professionals selected ESTs based on pre-determined criteria.

2. Based on the differences in their criteria, in which of the following ways are *well-established* treatments different than those classified as *probably efficacious?*

   A. Only probably efficacious treatments allowed the use of a single case design experiments.
   B. Only well-established treatments allowed studies comparing the treatment to a psychological placebo.
   C. Only well-established treatments required demonstration by at least two different, independent investigators or investigating teams.
   D. Only well-established treatments allowed studies comparing the treatment to a pill placebo.

   A. *Incorrect*: Both sets of criteria allowed use of single subject designs. Well-established treatments required a larger series than did probably efficacious (see II under Well-Established and III under Probably Efficacious).

B. *Incorrect*: Studies using comparison to psychological placebos were acceptable in both sets of criteria (see IA under Well-Established and II under Probably Efficacious).

C. *Correct*: One of the primary differences between treatments classified as well-established and those classified as probably efficacious is that well-established therapies have had their efficacy demonstrated by at least two different, independent investigators (see V under Well-Established).

D. *Incorrect*: Studies using comparison to pill placebos were acceptable in both sets of criteria (see IA under Well-Established and II under Probably Efficacious).

Chapter 2: How Are Empirically Supported Treatments Related to Evidence–Based Practice?

1. Which statement best summarizes the difference between empirically supported treatments (ESTs) and evidence-based practice (EBP)?

A. EBP and ESTs are two labels describing the same thing.

B. EBP focuses on therapeutic relationship factors, ESTs focus on the content of therapy.

C. EBP does not integrate research results, ESTs do.

D. EBP is broader in scope than ESTs.

A. *Incorrect*: ESTs refer to treatments whose efficacy has been demonstrated through clinical research, while EBP is a broader concept that considers several factors related to the delivery of effective psychotherapy.

B. *Incorrect*: EBP considers factors beyond the therapeutic relationship, including evidence of the treatment's efficacy and effectiveness.

C. *Incorrect*: EBP does consider and integrate the best available evidence supporting a therapy.

D. *Correct*: EBP is a broader concept that considers several factors related to the delivery of effective psychotherapy including research support, culture, client preference, and factors related to the therapist, client, and their relationship.

2. Although the effective delivery of an empirically informed psychological treatment plan involves consideration of several factors including those related to the client, the therapist, their relationship, and the interventions used, the written treatment plan, by its nature, places emphasis on describing which of the following?

A. The client factors

B. The relationship factors

C. The therapist factors
D. The treatment interventions
  A. *Incorrect*: Although client factors must be taken into account in the delivery of any treatment plan, they take less prominence in the written treatment plan than do descriptions of the interventions.
  B. *Incorrect*: Although relationship factors must be taken into account in the delivery of any treatment plan, they take less prominence in the written treatment plan than do descriptions of the interventions.
  C. *Incorrect*: Although relationship factors must be taken into account in the delivery of any treatment plan, they take less prominence in the written treatment plan than do descriptions of the interventions.
  D. *Correct*: Relative to other considerations important in the delivery of an evidence-based treatment plan, treatment plan writing places emphasis on the content of the therapy (e.g., client objectives and therapist interventions consistent with ESTs).

Chapter 3: What Are the Advantages of Using Empirically Supported Treatments?

1. The potential advantages of using ESTs are:
  A. Found across several levels of the psychotherapy service delivery system.
  B. Primarily for clinicians, through malpractice protection.
  C. Primarily for agencies, through improved business competitiveness.
  D. Primarily for clients, through the previous demonstration of efficacy.
    A. *Correct*: Advantages have been identified for various constituencies and interests including clients, therapists, agencies, and the profession.
    B. *Incorrect*: Advantages extend beyond this particular one for clinicians.
    C. *Incorrect*: Advantages extend beyond this particular one for agencies.
    D. *Incorrect*: Advantages extend beyond this particular one for clients.

2. One of the advantages of using ESTs is that it may help close the *scientist-practitioner gap*. The gap in this sense refers to what?
  A. The dissemination of clinical research findings to community treatment settings.
  B. The theoretical orientations of researchers and practitioners.
  C. The training backgrounds of researchers and practitioners
  D. The types of clinical problems seen in both settings.

A. *Correct*: The gap in this sense refers the observation that many treatments identified as efficacious through clinical research are not practiced prevalently across community treatment settings, generally suggesting a lack of effective dissemination.

B. *Incorrect*: Although some scientists and practitioners may differ in their orientations and this difference may influence their practices, others do not differ. The gap in this sense refers to a lack of effective dissemination, not to this potential mediator of it.

C. *Incorrect*: Although some scientists and practitioners may differ in training backgrounds and this difference may influence their practices, others do not differ. The gap in this sense refers to a lack of effective dissemination, not to this potential mediator of it.

D. *Incorrect*: Although complexity may differ between clinical research participants in some studies and community clients, in some studies they do not. The gap in this sense refers to a lack of effective dissemination, not to this potential mediator of it.

Chapter 4: What Are the Limitations of Identified Empirically Supported Treatments?

1. An investigator is developing a new psychotherapy and wants to see if it performs better than a wait-list control condition. This type of study is typically used in the process of establishing the therapy's . . .

A. Effectiveness
B. Efficacy
C. Transportability
D. Utility

    A. *Incorrect*: Effectiveness studies test the generalizability of efficacious treatments to real-world applications. This wait-list-control study tests in part whether the condition being treated will improve on its own or requires treatment to improve, and is a type of study often used initially in the course of testing the efficacy of a treatment.

    B. *Correct*: This wait-list-control study tests in part whether the condition being treated will improve on its own or requires treatment to improve, and is a type of study often used initially in the course of testing the efficacy of a treatment.

    C. *Incorrect*: Transportability is synonymous with generalizability and is the subject of effectiveness and utility studies.

    D. *Incorrect*: Utility is an extension of effectiveness and refers to the applicability, feasibility, and practical usefulness of an intervention in the local or specific setting where it is offered.

2. Which of the following best characterizes one of the criticisms of the evidence base supporting most ESTs?

    A. Effectiveness studies are overrepresented.

    B. Effectiveness studies are underrepresented.

    C. Efficacy studies are overrepresented.

    D. Efficacy studies are underrepresented.

        A. *Incorrect*: One of the criticisms of ESTs is that there are *not* enough (effectiveness) studies demonstrating the generalizability of their efficacy to community applications.

        B. *Correct*: One of the criticisms of ESTs is that there are *not* enough (effectiveness) studies demonstrating the generalizability of their efficacy to community applications.

        C. *Incorrect*: The underrepresentation of effectiveness studies, not the overrepresentation of efficacy studies, is the point of the criticism.

        D. *Incorrect*: While some may question the interpretation made from efficacy studies supporting ESTs, it is not the lack of them that is the point of the criticism.

Chapter 5: What Are the Six Steps in Building a Treatment Plan?

1. A psychotherapy treatment plan can be drawn up without a diagnosis. For example, a good case formulation can be the basis of therapy. Why is it important to consider the diagnosis when developing a plan that could be informed by ESTs?

    A. A diagnosis is necessary to judge response to the EST.

    B. It is not necessary to consider diagnosis in evidence-based treatment planning.

    C. Some ESTs were developed and studied using diagnosis as inclusion criteria.

    D. Treatment may require medication, which typically requires diagnosis to be specified.

        A. *Incorrect*: Although diagnostic criteria can be used to assess response to treatment, outcome of treatment can be measured in other ways as well.

        B. *Incorrect*: See C.

C. *Correct*: Many ESTs were developed for the treatment problems defined by a diagnosis. Knowing the diagnosis is particularly important in deciding whether an EST is applicable to a client.

D. *Incorrect*: Although diagnosis is important in determining medication choice, this question pertains to ESTs, which are empirically supported psychological treatments.

2. The statement, "Identify, challenge, and change biased self-talk supportive of depression" is an example of which of the following steps in a treatment plan?

A. A primary problem
B. A short-term objective
C. A symptom manifestation
D. A treatment intervention

A. *Incorrect*: The primary problem (step 1 in treatment planning) is the summary description, usually in diagnostic terms, of the client's primary problem.

B. *Correct*: This is a short-term objective (step 5 in treatment planning). It describes the desired actions of the client in the treatment plan.

C. *Incorrect*: Symptom manifestations (step 2 in treatment planning) describe the client's particular expression (i.e., manifestations or symptoms) of a problem.

D. *Incorrect*: A treatment intervention (step 6 in treatment planning) describes the therapist's actions designed to help the client achieve therapeutic objectives.

Chapter 6: How Do You Integrate Empirically Supported Treatments into Treatment Planning?

1. Which of the following best describes the practice of incorporating only selected objectives and interventions from ESTs in treatment planning?

A. It is an empirically supported way to tailor the EST to the client.
B. It is how ESTs should be integrated into a treatment plan.
C. It is recommended as a useful means to shorting treatment length.
D. It may not be an empirically supported use of ESTs.

A. *Incorrect*: Although components of some multimodal ESTs have demonstrated efficacy on their own (e.g., exposure for some anxiety disorders), selective use without empirical support for it risks delivering a treatment whose efficacy has not been established.

B. *Incorrect*: Selective use without empirical support is not recommended because it risks delivering a treatment whose efficacy has not been established.

C. *Incorrect*: Although delivering only part of an EST may shorten treatment length, it risks delivering a treatment whose efficacy has not been established.

D. *Correct*: Although components of some multimodal ESTs have demonstrated efficacy on their own (e.g., exposure for some anxiety disorders), selective use without empirical support for it risks delivering a treatment whose efficacy has not been established. Incorporating the objectives and interventions of the EST as it was delivered in the studies supporting its efficacy is the recommended approach.

2. The statement, "Engage the client in *behavioral activation* by scheduling activities that have a high likelihood for pleasure and mastery," is an example of which of the following steps in a treatment plan?

A. A primary problem

B. A short-term objective

C. A symptom manifestation

D. A treatment intervention

    A. *Incorrect*: The statement describes the actions of the therapist, and is therefore an intervention. Depression is likely to be the "problem" in this example.

    B. *Incorrect*: The statement describes the actions of the therapist, and is therefore an intervention. Objectives describe client actions.

    C. *Incorrect*: The statement describes the actions of the therapist, and is therefore an intervention. Sadness is an example of a "symptom manifestation" for depression.

    D. *Correct*: The statement describes the actions of the therapist, and is therefore an intervention.

STUDY PACKAGE
CONTINUING EDUCATION
CREDIT INFORMATION

Evidence-Based Psychotherapy Treatment Planning

Our goal is to provide you with current, accurate and practical information from the most experienced and knowledgeable speakers and authors.

Listed below are the continuing education credit(s) currently available for this self-study package. *Please note: Your state licensing board dictates whether self study is an acceptable form of continuing education. Please refer to your state rules and regulations.*

COUNSELORS: PESI, LLC is recognized by the National Board for Certified Counselors to offer continuing education for National Certified Counselors. Provider #: 5896. We adhere to NBCC Continuing Education Guidelines. This self-study package qualifies for 1.0 contact hours.

SOCIAL WORKERS: PESI, LLC, 1030, is approved as a provider for continuing education by the Association of Social Work Boards, 400 South Ridge Parkway, Suite B, Culpeper, VA 22701. www.aswb.org. Social workers should contact their regulatory board to determine course approval. Course Level: All Levels. Social Workers will receive 1.0 (Clinical) continuing education clock hours for completing this self-study package.

PSYCHOLOGISTS: PESI, LLC is approved by the American Psychological Association to sponsor continuing education for psychologists. PESI, LLC maintains responsibility for these materials and their content. PESI is offering these self-study materials for 1.0 hours of continuing education credit.

ADDICTION COUNSELORS: PESI, LLC is a Provider approved by NAADAC Approved Education Provider Program. Provider #: 366. This self-study package qualifies for 1.0 contact hours.

MARRIAGE & FAMILY THERAPISTS: This activity consists of 1.0 clock hours of continuing education instruction. Credit requirements and approvals vary per state board regulations. Please save the course outline, the certificate of completion you receive from the activity and contact your state board or organization to determine specific filing requirements.

NURSES/NURSE PRACTITIONERS/CLINICAL NURSE SPECIALISTS: This independent study package meets the criteria for a formally approved American Nurses Credentialing Center (ANCC) Activity . PESI, LLC is an approved provider by the American Psychological Association, which is recognized by the ANCC for behavioral health related activities.

Nurses completing these learner-directed materials will earn 1.1 contact hours.

Procedures:

1. Review the workbook that contains the written materials.

2. Review and study the recording.

3. If seeking credit, the following must be completed on the post-test/evaluation form:

> -Complete post test/evaluation in entirety; including your email address to receive your certificate much faster versus by mail.
> -Upon completion, mail to the address listed on the form, or fax to 1-800-554-9775, "Attention: CE Dept".

Your completed post test/evaluation will be graded. If you receive a passing score (70% and above), you will be emailed/faxed/mailed a certificate of successful completion with earned continuing education credits. (Please write your email address on the post test/ evaluation form for fastest response.) If you do not pass the post-test, you will be sent a letter indicating areas of deficiency, and another post test to complete. The post-test must be resubmitted and receive a passing grade before credit can be awarded. We will allow you to re-take as many times as necessary to receive a certificate.

If you have any questions, please feel free to contact our customer service department at 1.800.844.8260.

Course Content

This Workbook is a supplement to the Evidence-Based Treatment Planning DVD, which is focused on informing mental health clinicians and addiction counselors about evidence-based psychological treatment. The content in the DVD and workbook will examine the following: History of the Empirically Supported Treatment (EST) Movement, EST and Evidence-Based Practice (EBP), Advantages of Using ESTs, Limitations of ESTs, Essential Elements of Treatment Planning, Empirically informed treatment Planning.

PESI LLC
PO BOX 1000
Eau Claire, WI 54702-1000

Evidence-Based Psychotherapy Treatment Planning

PO BOX 1000
Eau Claire, WI 54702
800-844-8260

Any persons interested in receiving credit may photocopy this form, complete and return with a payment of $15.00 per person CE fee. A certificate of successful completion will be sent to you. To receive your certificate sooner than two weeks, rush processing is available for a fee of $10. Please attach check or include credit card information below.

Mail to: PESI, PO Box 1000, Eau Claire, WI 54702 or fax to PESI (800) 554-9775 (both sides)

CE Fee: $15: (Rush processing fee: $10)   **Total to be charged** _____

Credit Card #: _____ **Exp Date:** _____ **V-Code*:** _____
(*MC/VISA/Discover: last 3-digit # on signature panel on back of card.) (*American Express: 4-digit # above account # on face of card.)

	LAST	FIRST	M.I.

Name (please print): _____ _____ _____

Address: _____ Daytime Phone: _____

City: _____ State: _____ Zip Code: _____

Signature: _____ Email: _____

Date Completed: _____ Actual time (# of hours) taken to complete this offering: _____hours

Program Objectives After completing this publication, I have been able to achieve these objectives:

Examine how empirically supported psychological treatments have been identified	Yes	No
Compare the distinction between empirically supported treatments and an evidence-based practice	Yes	No
State the advantages of using empirically supported treatments as part of an evidence-based practice	Yes	No
Define limitations of empirically supported treatments	Yes	No
Identify what the clinician can do to obtain the goal of having an evidence-based practice	Yes	No
List the six steps in building a clear psychotherapy treatment plan	Yes	No
Explain the process of constructing a psychotherapy treatment plan and informing it with empirically supported treatments	Yes	No

PESI LLC
PO BOX 1000
Eau Claire, WI 54702-1000

ZNT042100

CE Release Date: 3/30/10

Participant Profile:
1. Job Title: _____ Employment setting: _____

1. How were empirically supported treatments (ESTs) identified originally by Division 12 of the American Psychological Association (APA's Division 12)?
a. Task groups assessed the treatment preferences of a sample of patients.
b. Task groups reviewed the practice patterns clinical researchers.
c. Task groups reviewed the treatment outcome literature using pre-determined EST
criteria.
d. Task groups surveyed the clinical practice patterns of expert therapists.

2. Under what two labels did APA's Division 12 categorize ESTs?
a. Well-established and established.
b. Well-established and unestablished.
c. Well-established and probably efficacious.
d. Well-established and efficacious.

3. The statement, "The integration of the best available research with clinical expertise, in the context of patient characteristics, culture, and preferences" represents which of the following?
a. The definition of an empirically supported treatment (EST).
b. The definition of an evidence-based practice (EBP).
c. The definition of an efficacious treatment.
d. The definition of an effective treatment.

4. The criteria used by the APA's Division 12 task group to identify empirically supported treatments placed emphasis on what types of studies?
a. Effectiveness.
b. Efficacy.
c. Qualitative.
d. Utility.

5. An investigator is studying whether a treatment that has shown efficacy in one setting can be used successfully in another setting. Which of the following best describes this type of study?
a. Effectiveness.
b. Efficacy.
c. Qualitative.
d. Quantitative.

6. In this program, which of the following was noted as an advantage to identifying and using ESTs?
a. They increase client confidence that there will be a positive treatment benefit.
b. They all have the same level of evidence to show their efficacy and utility.
c. They are easier to learn than other treatment approaches.
d. They consistently perform better than medication.

7. In this program, which of the following was noted as a limitation of some well-established ESTs?
a. Randomization procedures in these trials have been flawed.
b. Studies demonstrating their effectiveness in community applications are relatively few.
c. Independent investigators or investigative teams have not demonstrated their efficacy.
d. The treatment procedures are unclear because manuals were not used to guide the therapy.

8. Which of the following was described as the first step in psychotherapy treatment planning?
a. Creating short-term objectives.
b. Identifying the primary problem.
c. Selecting therapeutic interventions.
d. Specifying long-term goals.

9. The approach to empirically informing psychotherapy treatment planning described in this program includes integrating objectives and therapeutic interventions consistent with those of identified ESTs.

TRUE   FALSE

10. Although APA's Division 12 was at the forefront of the movement to identify ESTs in America, there are other reliable sources of information on evidence-based psychotherapy practices available to practitioners.

TRUE   FALSE

PESI LLC
PO BOX 1000
Eau Claire, WI 54702-1000